Swearing People

SwearWord
Adult Coloring Book

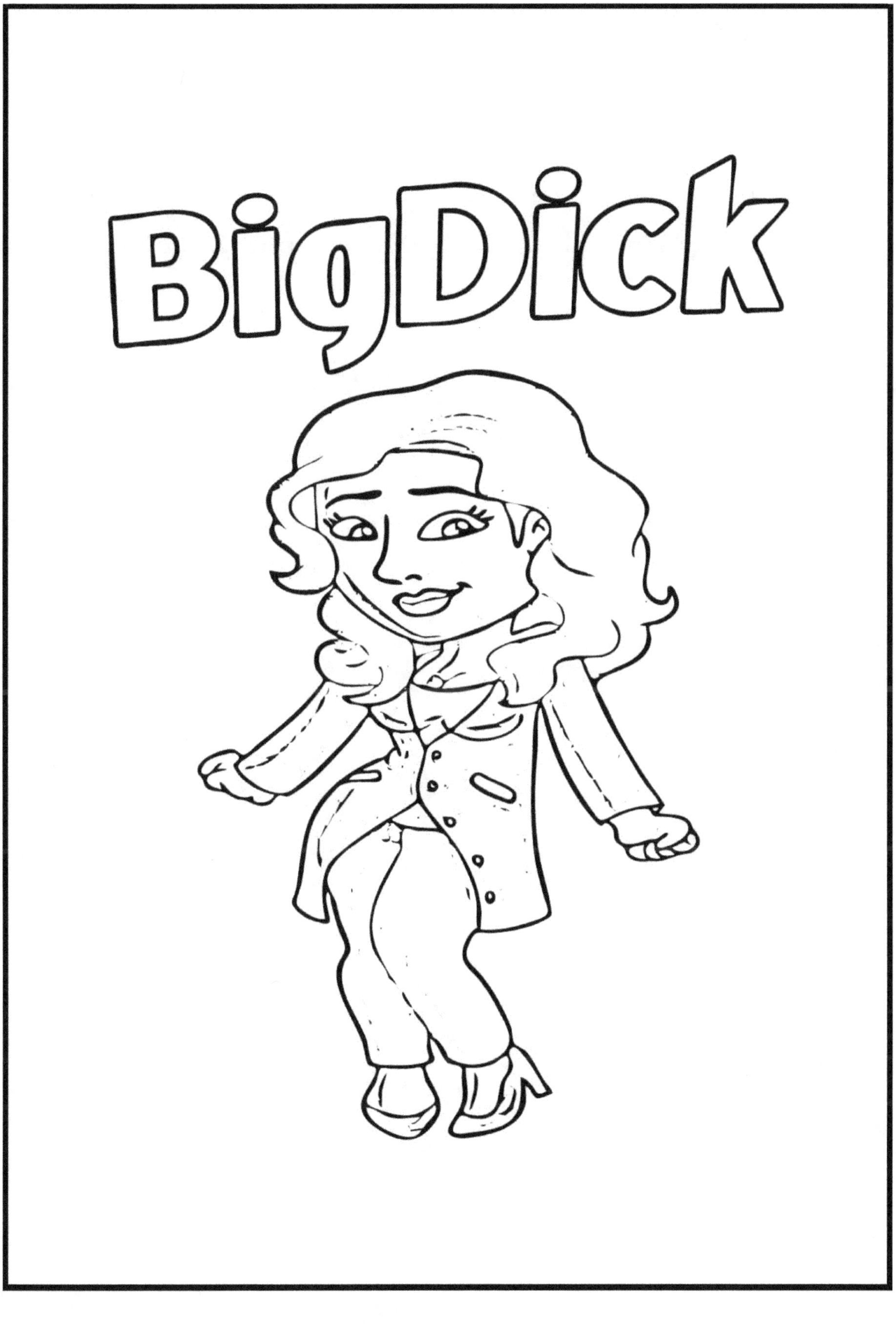
BigDick

AssHat

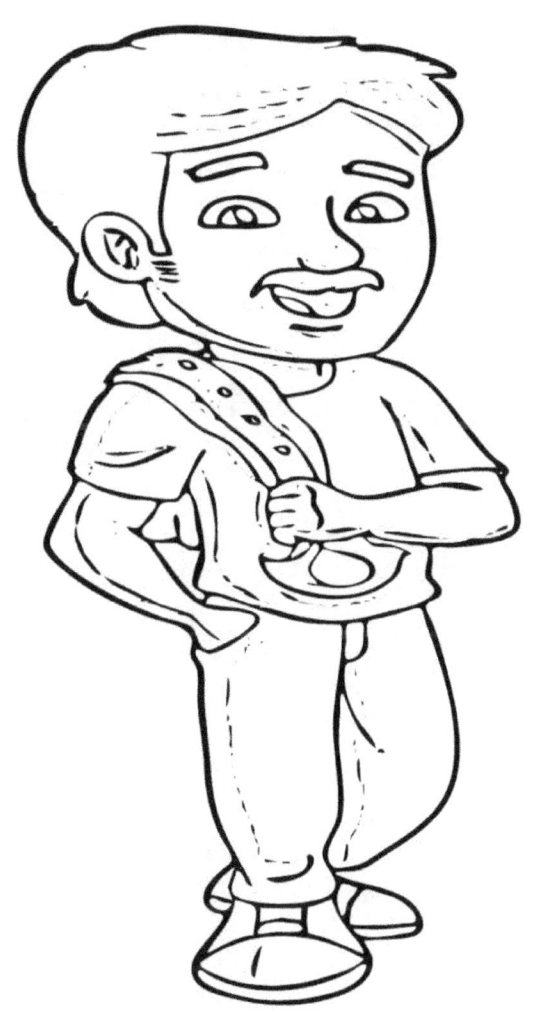

JizzStain

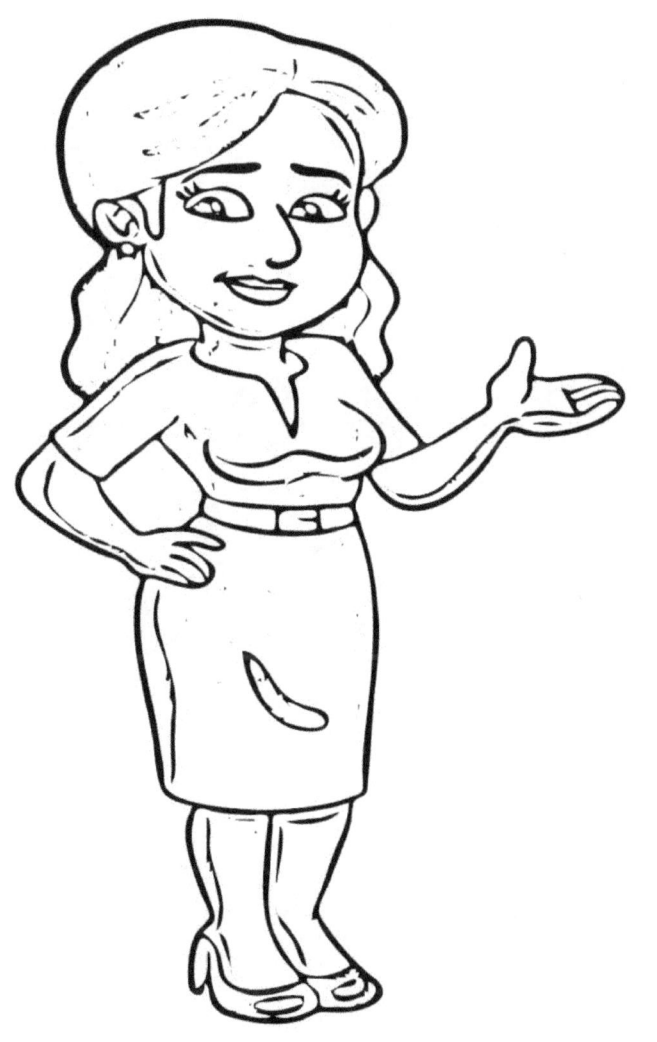

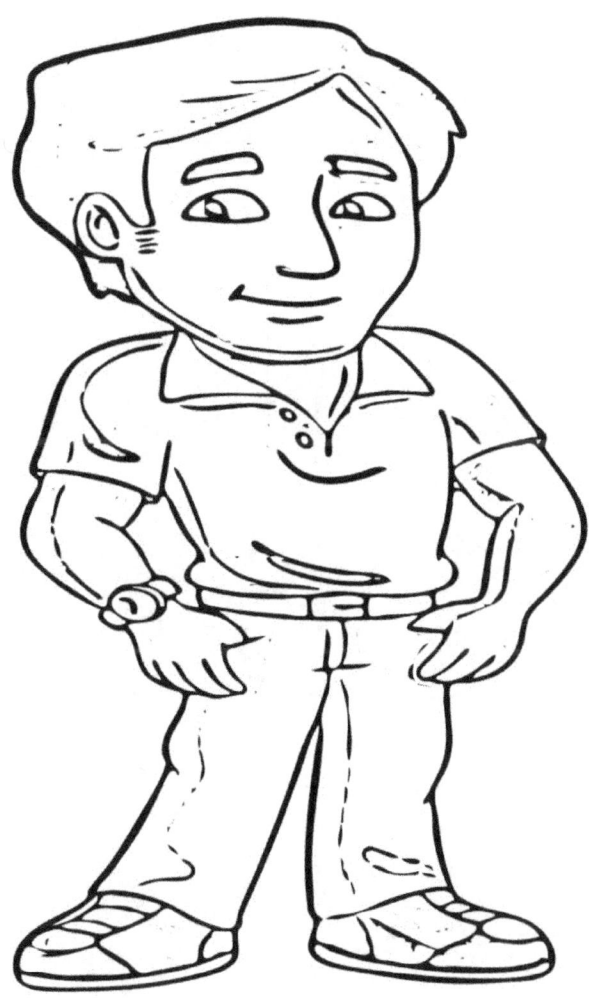

TittySpank

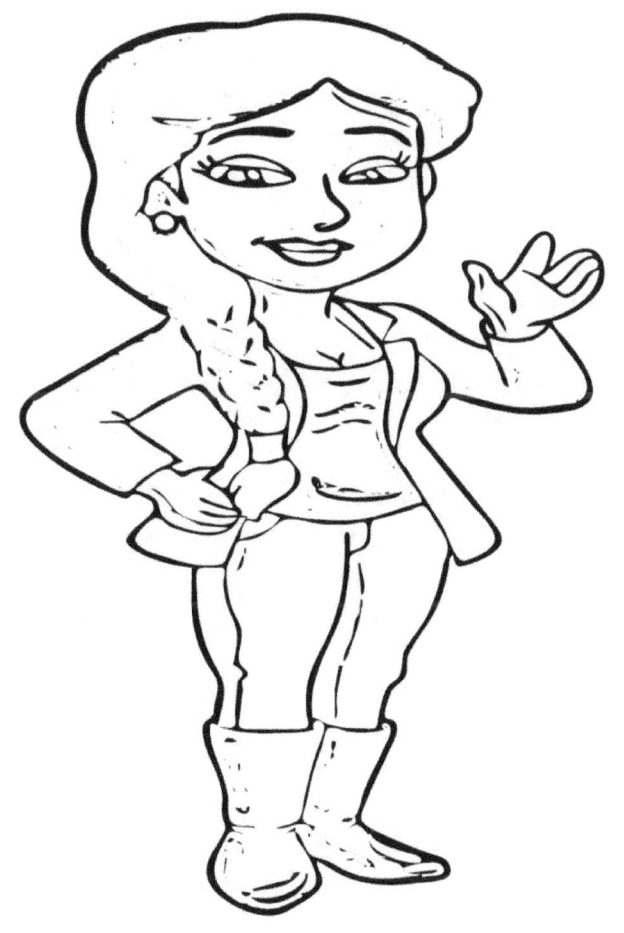

ButtMunch

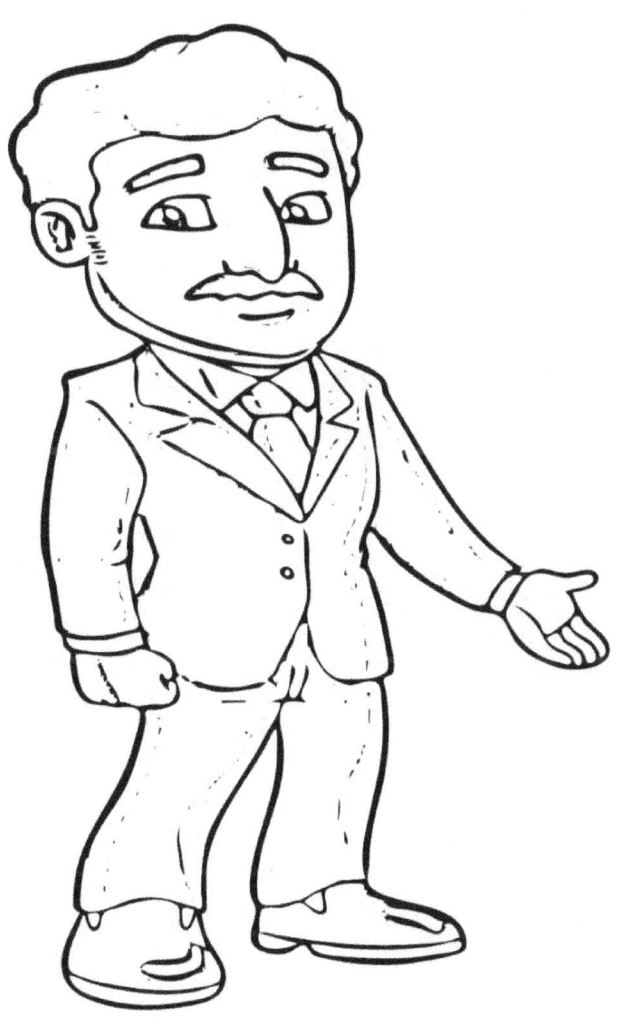

CockJuice

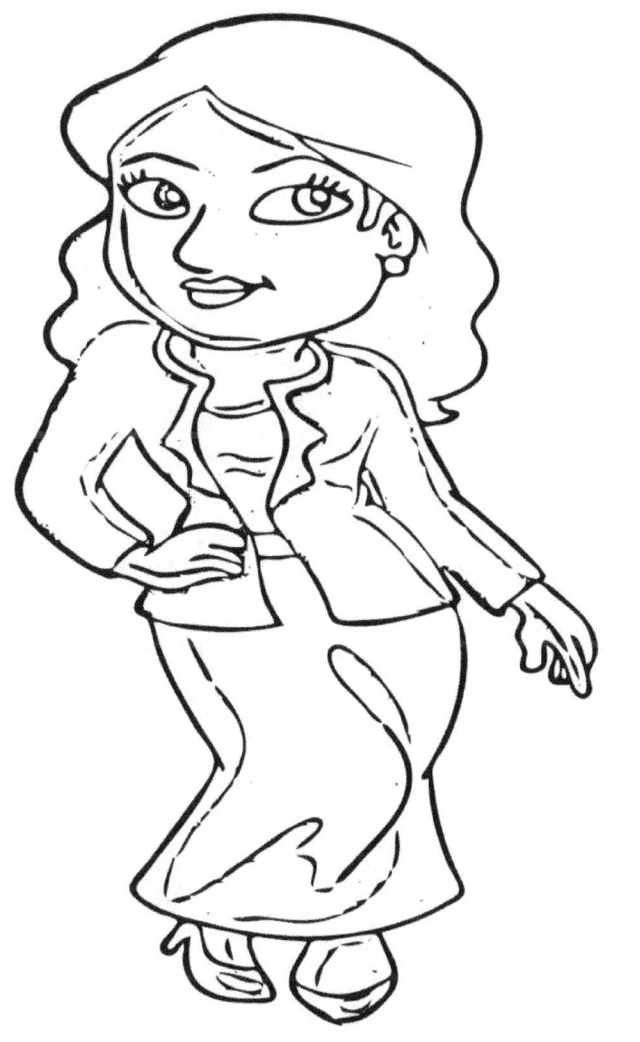

Cum Depository

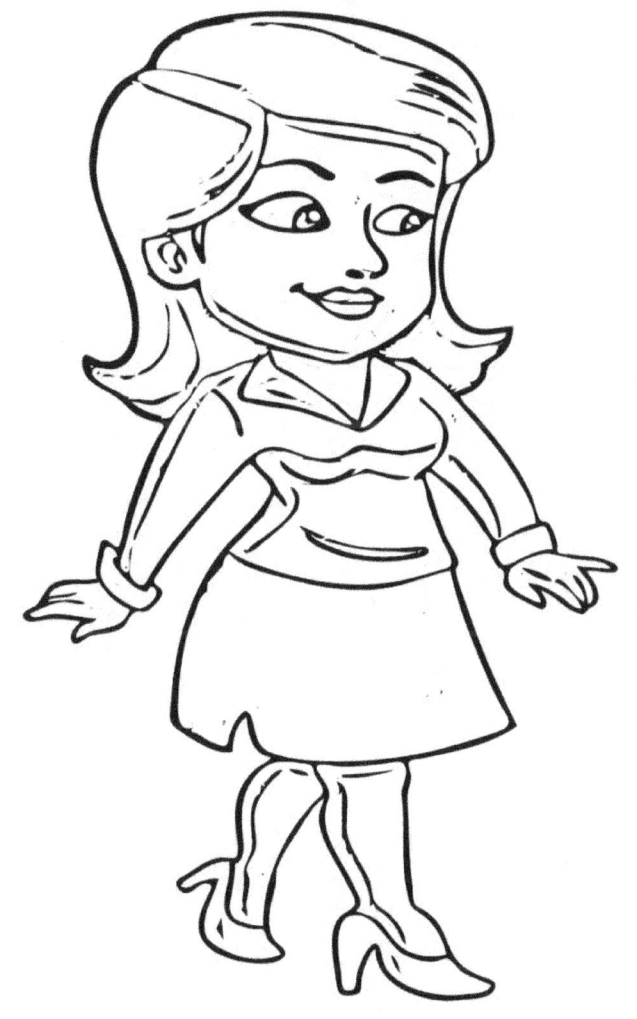

FuckButter

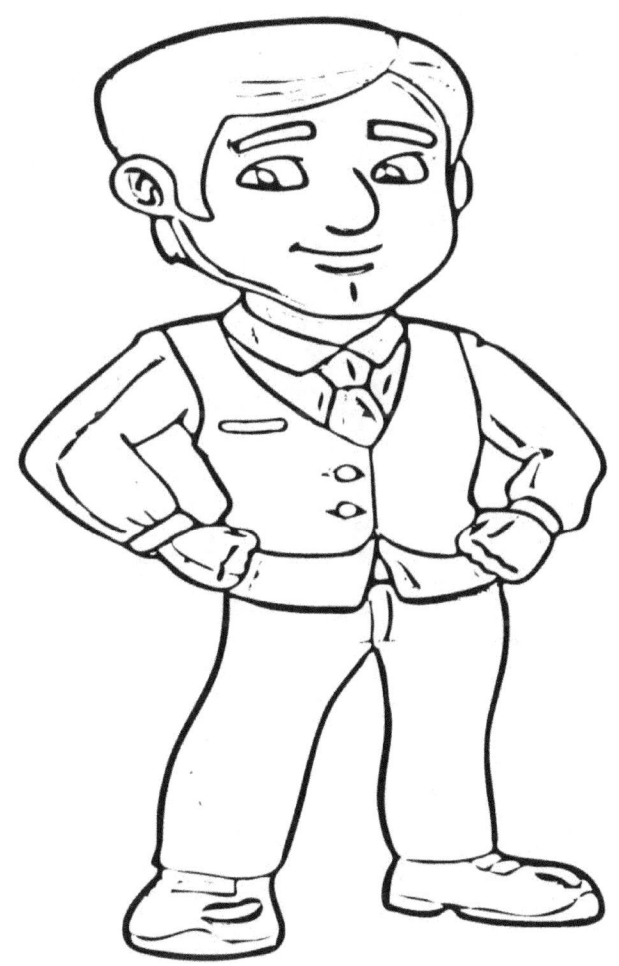

Spaghetti Girth

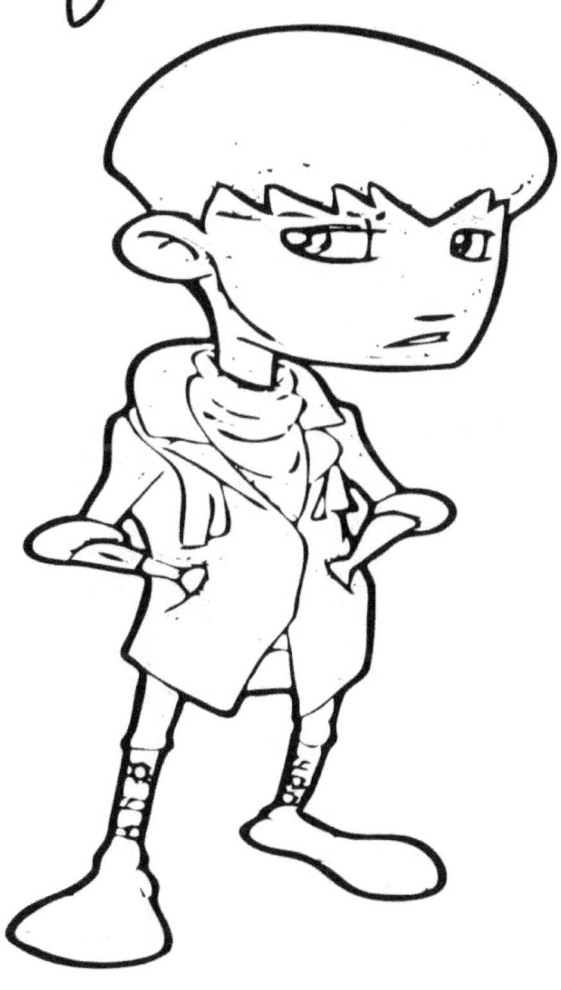

Anal Tycoon

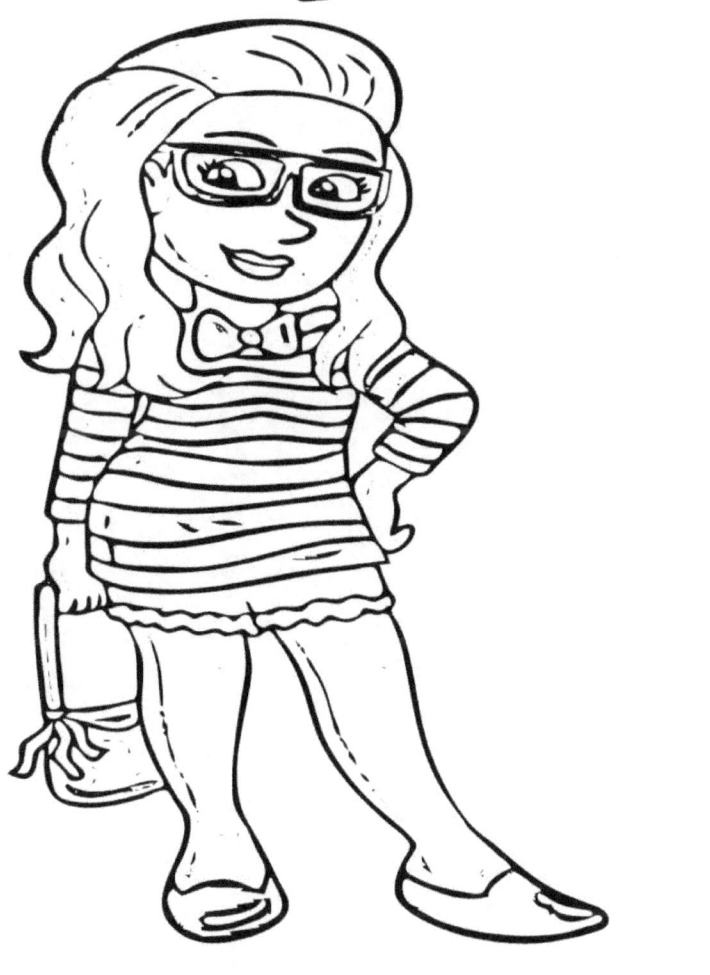

Bell-End

SackRider

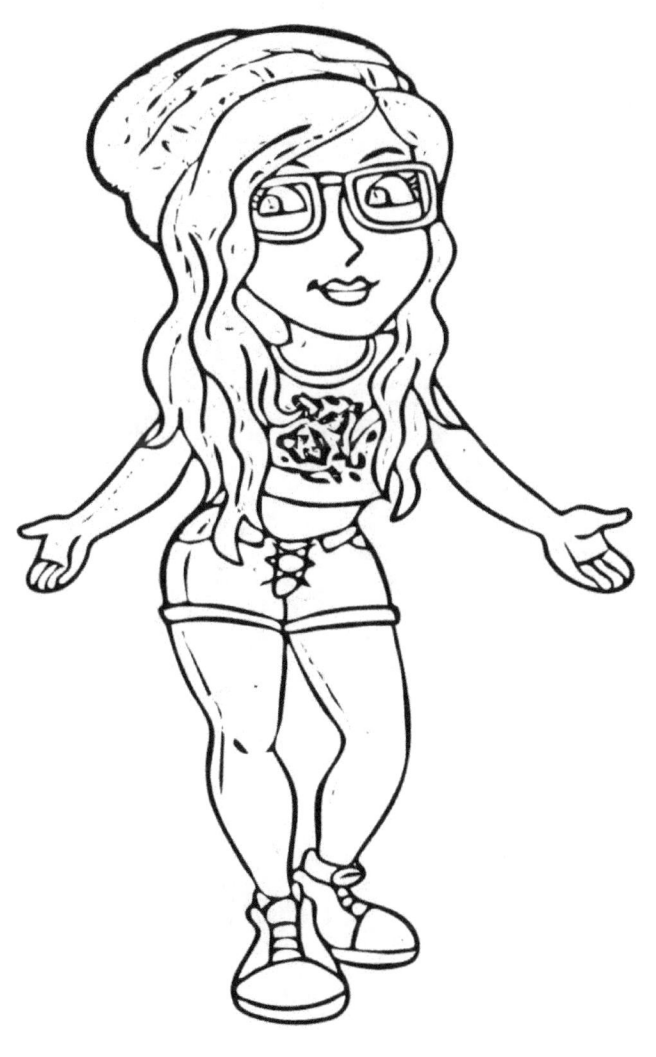

SquirtLips

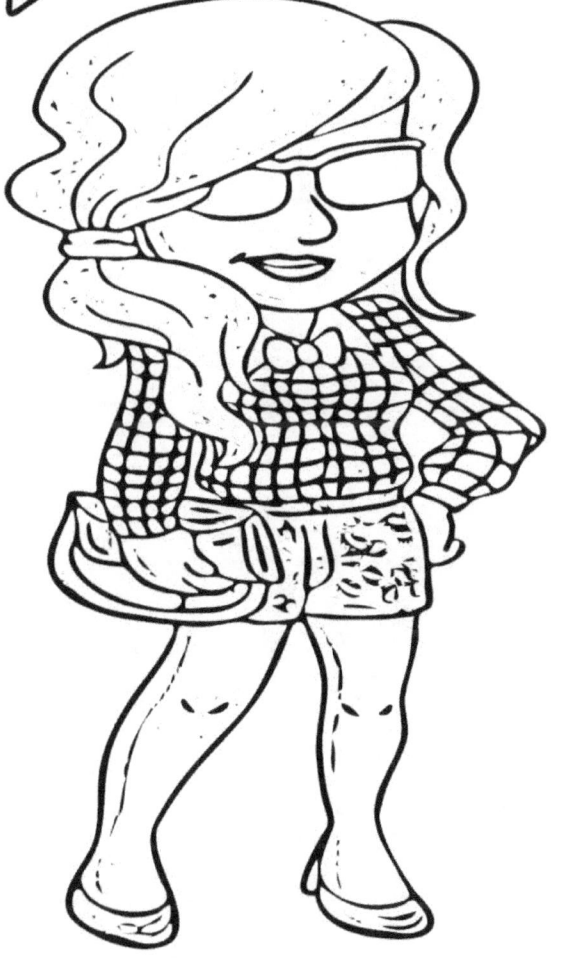

Beefy 'Nads

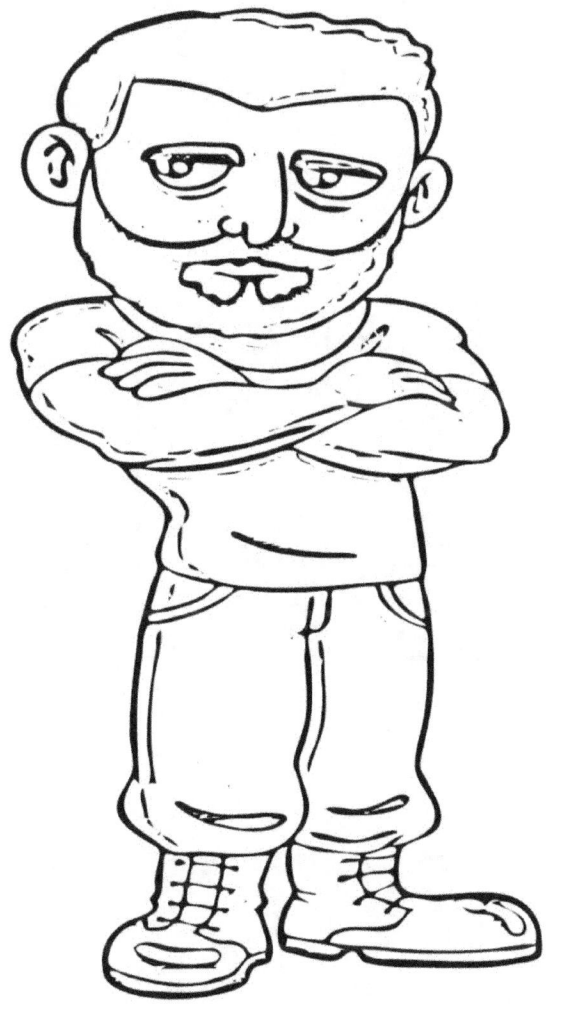

QuimCake

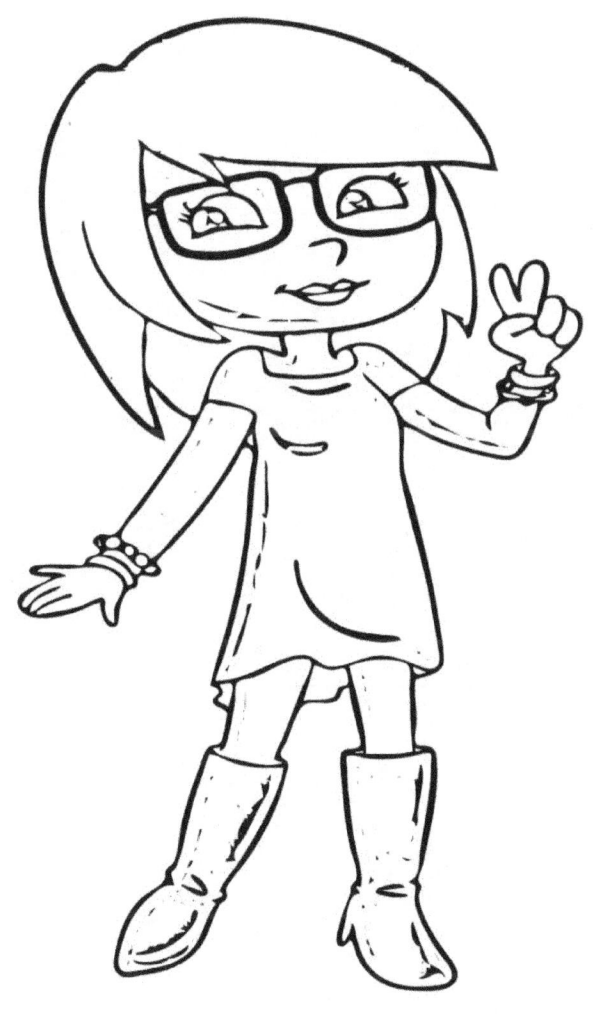

DonkeyDong

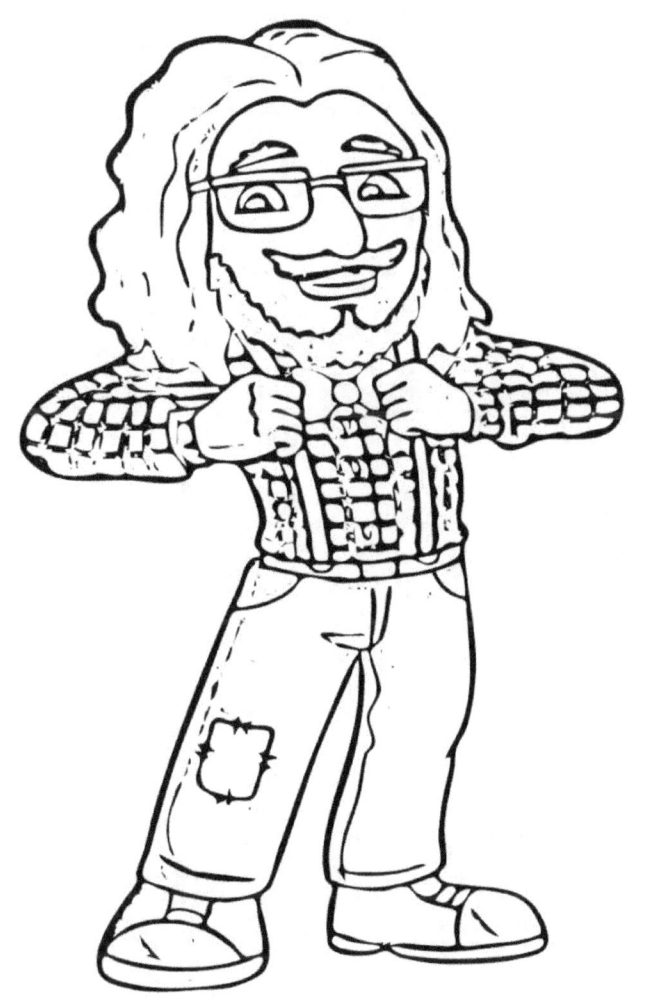

TwatWaffle

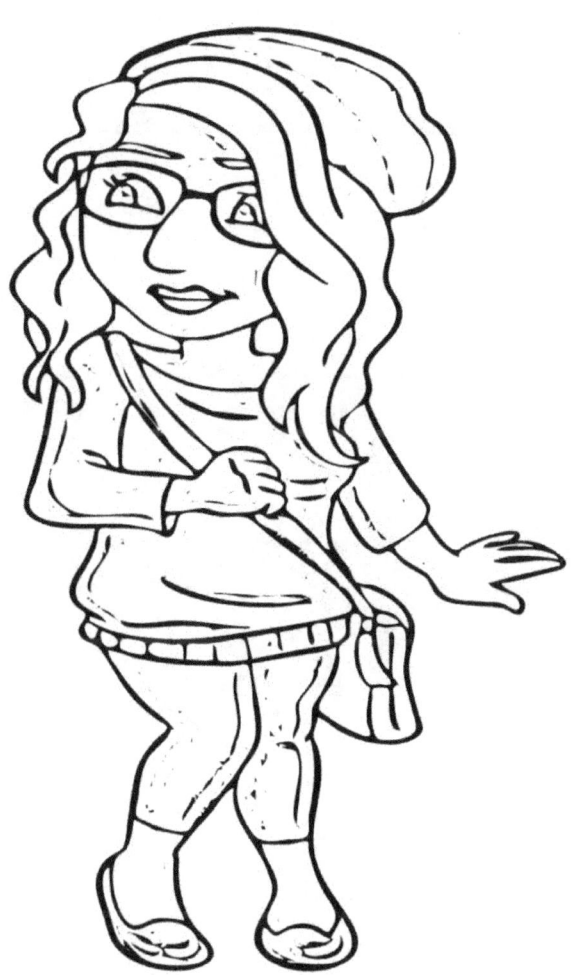

FurBurger

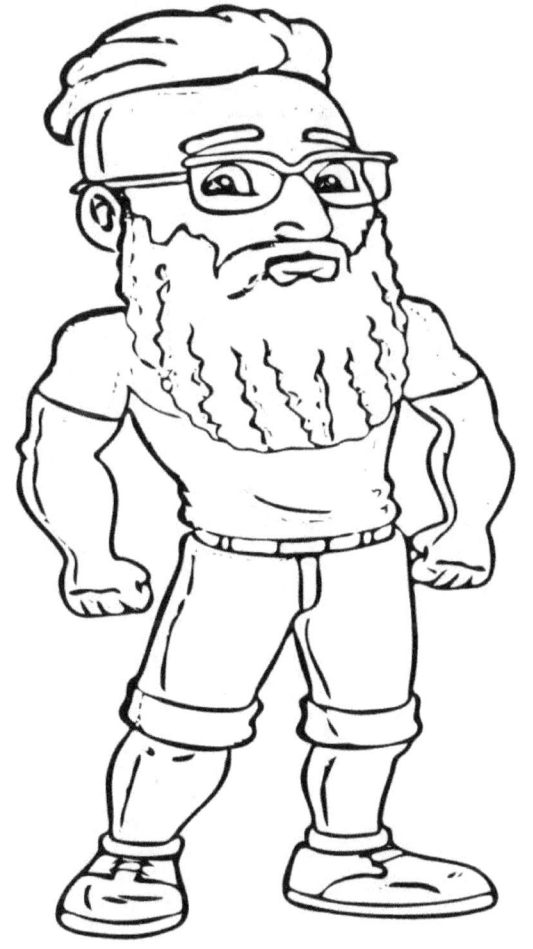

ToolMaster

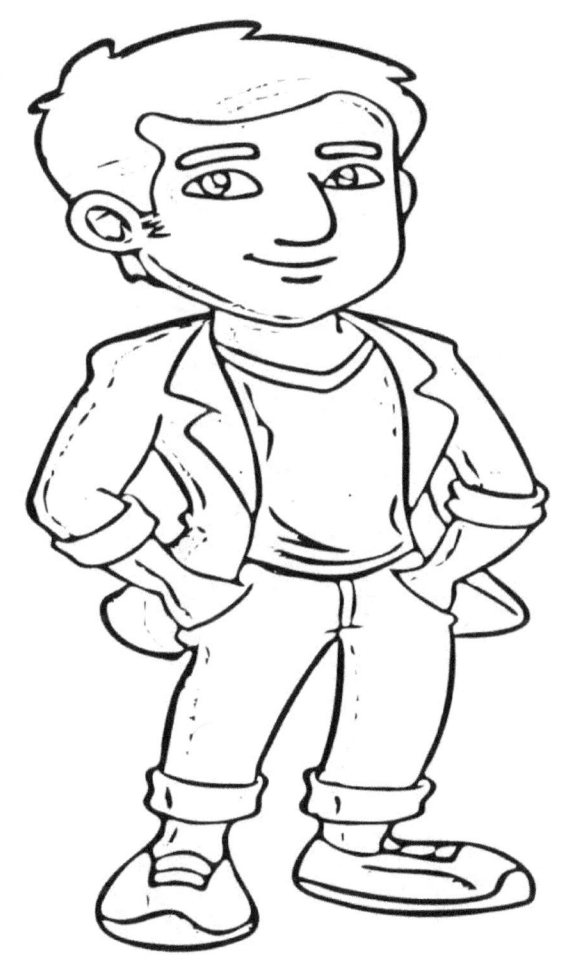